MARY QUEEN OF SCOTS

A Life from Beginning to End

Copyright © 2016 by Hourly History

D1457401

Table of Contents

Early Life
A Fairy Tale in France
A Most Tragic Year
Return to Scotland and Marriage to Darnley
The Murders of Rizzio and Darnley
The Final Rebellion
Elizabeth and the Casket Letters
An Incarcerated Queen
The Execution

Introduction

Mary Queen of Scots is one of the great celebrities of the British monarchy. Everyone knows the story of Mary's tumultuous life or some version of it, and her tomb at Westminster Abbey remains one of the most visited tourist sites in London.

Born into a powerful royal dynasty that was already at the heart of the religious and political war between European nations intent on destroying each other, Mary's life was never destined to be easy. Born and raised to be the queen of not one but potentially three different nations, Mary fit the part of a great monarch in her looks, intelligence, and wit; by the time she reached her wedding day, her future looked brighter than the rising sun.

But the tragic events of Mary's adulthood eclipsed those of her happy childhood. As Mary's support system disintegrated, she sought solace in the arms of disloyal men; she was betrayed time and time again. Unable to hold together her fatally unstable country, Mary failed to maintain her grip on the ever-tottering crown on her head and was finally removed from the Scottish throne by an armed rebellion.

To her champions, Mary was a victim of the Scottish lords and French and English politicians who constantly plotted her demise, but to her critics, she was an ineffectual queen, ruled by her emotions and more concerned with her love affairs than repairing her fractured country.

There was far more to Mary Queen of Scots than meets the eye, and this book is an attempt to see past the legends to get a glimpse of a woman who once held the fate of three kingdoms in the palm of her hand.

Chapter One

Early Life

"Who that intendeth France to win, with Scotland let him begin."

—Popular 16th-century English rhyme

Mary Stuart was born at Linlithgow on either the 7th or the 8th of December 1542 and was the child of James V, King of Scots, and his wife, Mary of Guise. Mary and James had already lost two sons in infancy; as Mary was premature, they feared they may lose her too, so she was baptized almost immediately at the Church of St. Michael.

Mary was a fighter, and proved herself in the very first week of her life: she not only survived but, at just six days old, took the throne of her father and became Mary Queen of Scots. The exact cause of James V's death at the age of thirty is unclear. Some historians point to the Scottish defeat at the Battle of Solway Moss and conclude that James faded away from depression, while others note that he may have drank contaminated water while on campaign. Either way, James' death was abrupt and untimely and left Mary as the only legitimate heir to survive him.

From the first week of her life, Mary Queen of Scots was a source of discord in Scotland, England, and even Europe. Mary's mother, Mary of Guise, was a powerful player in the House of Guise, a French noble family that was heavily involved in the politics of 16th century France. At the time, public opinion in Scotland was very much divided over French influence in Scotland, with some favoring an alliance with England over an alliance with

France. As the child of Mary of Guise, Mary represented French interests, but as the great-niece of the infamous King Henry VIII of England, Mary also had strong ties to the English.

Scotland's split between supporters of England and supporters of France was further complicated by religion. In 1542, England was not yet Protestant, but it was certainly heading that way – meanwhile, France was resolutely Catholic. Scotland was also still Catholic, but many noble families had been watching Henry VIII carefully as he rejected the authority of the Pope and broke away from the Roman Catholic Church. Henry's reformed Church of England was winning converts, even in Scotland, and many noblemen were made rich beyond their dreams as he redistributed the spoils of the church amongst his allies.

A popular English rhyme of the time quipped, "who that intendeth France to win, with Scotland let him begin." Henry VIII is said to have enjoyed quoting the rhyme himself, making clear his intention to dominate France by way of Scotland.

As Mary was a newborn when she inherited the throne of Scotland, the country was initially ruled by regents. Mary's mother, Mary of Guise, was not permitted to rule as regent, but remained Mary's protector; the role of regent fell to the next in succession, James Hamilton, second Earl of Arran and great-grandson of King James II of Scotland. Hamilton was thought to be a poor leader and was easily influenced by both pro-English and pro-French politicians, often adding fuel to the fire of the countries' conflicts.

Little has been recorded in the early years of Mary's childhood, but the first few years of her life were dominated by some political machinations that would decide her future husband. With Hamilton in place as regent, Henry VIII saw his opportunity to detach Scotland from France and further English interests in the country that bordered his own. Henry proposed a future marriage between Mary and his own infant son Edward, who was not yet six years old, in an attempt to force an allegiance. In 1543, when Mary was six months old, Hamilton accepted Henry's offer and had the Treaty of Greenwich drawn up to seal the deal.

The Treaty of Greenwich stipulated that Mary should be taken to England where, at the age of ten, she and Edward would marry, and Henry could have a hand in her upbringing. This plan showed Henry's clear intention of incorporating Scotland into the Kingdom of England and caused pro-French factions led by Cardinal Beaton to intervene. The treaty was rejected, and Hamilton revealed that he thought his own son, the Master of Hamilton, would make a better husband for Mary than the English Prince Edward.

With a conflict with England now in the cards, an army of Cardinal Beaton's supporters escorted the child Queen and her mother to Stirling Castle on 27th July 1543. On the 9th September of that year, Mary was crowned queen.

Henry VIII was furious, and shortly before Mary's coronation, ordered the arrest of Scottish merchants heading for France. These illegal arrests caused much anger in Scotland and served only to intensify pro-French Scots hatred of the English. Once the Treaty of Greenwich had been officially rejected by the Parliament of Scotland, Henry resorted to a brutal military campaign to force the marriage of Mary and his son Edward. What the Scots referred to as a "rough wooing" was actually a series of English-led raids that saw the border abbeys of Kelso, Jedburgh, Melrose and Dryburgh burned to the ground. Soon after, in May 1546, Cardinal Beaton was murdered in St Andrew's Castle.

Henry VIII died in January 1547, but his campaign against the Scots was taken up immediately by his next in line, the Duke of Somerset, acting as Lord Protector to his infant son Edward. The Duke led an army north and defeated the Scots at the Battle of Pinkie Cleugh. Unable to take much more harassment from English forces, and desperate to protect their infant Queen, the Scots turned to the French for help.

Chapter Two

A Fairy Tale in France

"One of the most perfect creatures that ever was seen, such a one as from this very young age with its wondrous and estimable beginnings has raised such expectations that it isn't possible to hope for more from a princess on this earth."

—Jean de Beaugue

Hamilton was easily convinced that the safest place for Mary was under the protection of France. Even the Earl of Angus, commander of the Scottish forces at the Battle of Pinkie and a committed Anglophile, knew that the France was Scotland's best hope against the English. Pleased with the turn of events, Henry II, King of France, demanded that Mary be brought to France and betrothed to his own son, Dauphin Francis. In return, Henry promised he would provide Scotland with 6,000 troops to fight the English. Hamilton agreed to the arrangement, and in June 1548 French armed support arrived in Scotland to take back the English-held town of Haddington. The marriage treaty was agreed by Scottish Parliament on 7th July 1548, and on the 29th July Mary set sail for France.

As she boarded Henry II's own royal galley, she was watched by one of her French protectors, Jean de Beaugue, who later wrote that she was "one of the most perfect creatures that ever was seen, such a one as from this very young age with its wondrous and estimable beginnings has raised such expectations that it isn't possible to hope for more from a princess on this earth."

Mary's childhood at the French court is the stuff of fairy tales. Still just five years old, Mary arrived in France with a personal entourage of Scots to help her settle in. Mary's illegitimate half-brother Lord James Stewart, Lady Fleming, Mary of Guise's closest confidante, Lords Erskine and Livingston, Janet Sinclair, Mary's nurse, and the "four Marys", her four best friends all named Mary, made up the bulk of her company.

The crossing from Dumbarton in England to Saint-Pol-de-Léon in Brittany was long and gruelling, and on arrival, Mary was welcomed by her grandparents, Claude Duke of Guise and Antoinette of Bourbon. From the moment she was first received by the French court, little Mary caused a sensation. Henry II led an unusual household, with his wife Catherine de' Medici, and his mistress Diane de Poitiers, living in harmony; Diane even had a hand in the education of Henry and Catherine's four children. It was agreed in a memo from Henry, before Mary's arrival, that Mary would receive precedence over all of Henry's children apart from the Dauphin, and that Mary should "walk ahead of my daughters because her marriage to my son is agreed, and on top of that she is a crowned Queen."

It was agreed early on that Mary would be educated alongside Henry's children. This was a break with tradition and offered a number of benefits to the French king. On her arrival, Mary spoke only Scots and no French, something that had to be set right immediately and would ensure the Scottish queen would always feel that France was her home away from home. Also, Mary's male attendants were poorly received by the French court, and Henry wanted to send those officers that had entered Mary's service in Scotland home in order to raise her as though she was his own daughter. The other three "Marys" were sent to a local convent school to be educated, and only Lady Fleming seemed secure in her position as Mary's governess, although it soon emerged that Lady Fleming had become Henry's latest lover.

Despite the complexities of the French King's domestic arrangements, Mary flourished in France and was much-loved by all. Described as having auburn hair and a fine, light complexion, Mary was a beautiful young Queen and said to be graceful and self-assured. Mary was also charming and intelligent, and became fluent in French, both written and spoken, in less than two years. In later years she added Italian, Latin, Spanish, and Greek to her list of languages spoken, and became proficient in playing lute and virginals, writing prose and poetry, horsemanship and falconry.

It is said that Mary and her future husband Dauphin Francis got on well together from the very first day they met. Mary was tall for her age, especially for the time, and by the time she was an adult, she was around five feet 11 inches tall. She and Francis, who was a small child, first danced together at Mary's "coming out" a few days after her arrival in France. The event was the marriage between Mary's Uncle Francis and Anne d'Este, Duke of Ferrara, and all of Europe's finest noblemen were in attendance. Henry used this opportunity to draw attention to his new daughter, the "Queen of Scotland", and Mary rose to the occasion beautifully.

While Mary enjoyed all the pomp and ceremony of the French royal court politics, Scotland became ever more unsettled. Between 1553 and 1558, Henry Tudor's eldest child, Mary Tudor, was Queen of England, and had aggressively set about restoring the Roman Catholic Church using methods that would later give her the sobriquet "Bloody Mary". In 1554, Mary married Prince Philip of Spain, who boasted that for every fort built by the French in Scotland, he would construct three more on the

English side of the border. Battle lines between England and Scotland were being drawn.

It was decided that in order to exert more influence, Mary Queen of Scots should be declared "of age," despite the fact that she was just eleven years old. The usual age of majority for a royal minor was between 15 and 18 years old, but Mary's advisors urged her to take up her rights as queen to cast out the ineffectual Hamilton, Earl of Arran. At the same time, Mary of Guise, Mary's mother, was unhappy with her diminishing power in Scotland; she challenged Hamilton, Earl of Arran for the regency she believed belonged to her. She was successful, and on the 12th of April 1554, Mary of Guise became the regent of Scotland - much to the eleven-year-old Queen Mary's delight. Mary wrote a letter of congratulations to her mother using the words, " *la Royne, ma mere.*"

Henry II of France had publicly proclaimed France and Scotland to be "one country", a presumptive statement given Mary and Francis were yet to be married, and one that raised the real possibility that Scotland could become a French satellite land or even be incorporated into France as the Duchy of Brittany had been in 1494. Furthermore, Mary of Guise's regency depended heavily on the protection of French troops stationed in Scotland. Many Scots viewed the French presence as an occupation, and Protestant reformers continued to gain strength, claiming to be the only faction to stay patriotic to the Scottish crown.

Chapter Three

A Most Tragic Year

"All that I can tell you is that I account myself one of the happiest women in the world."

—Mary Queen of Scots and Queen Consort of France

A number of important events took place in 1558. On the 1st January 1558, the Duke of Guise led a French attack on the town of Calais. The town had an old-fashioned castle and was all but undefended, and the town was easily taken by the French. King Henry II of France was elated with the recovery of Calais from the English and led a victorious procession through the town.

Mary was married on the 24th April 1558, in an event as spectacular as you would expect to mark the union of the Queen of Scotland and future King of France. On the morning of her wedding, Mary wrote to her mother of her excitement, saying, "All I can tell you is that I account myself one of the happiest women in the world." The wedding took place at the Cathedral of Notre-Dame; crowds of French men, women, and children came out to bear witness to the special day. With an elaborate ceremony, endless banquets, an opulent ball, and numerous processions, Mary's wedding day was a dream from start to finish, and it was agreed that Mary and Francis made the perfect dynastic match. The wedding made Francis King Consort of Scotland and together the King and Queen were set to unite the crowns of France, Scotland, and England as one, shaping a dynasty that would come to dominate the whole of Europe.

Before her wedding, Mary had signed two important documents. In one, she had promised the Scottish people that despite her union with France, Scotland would remain independent. Mary promised to observe "the freedoms, liberties and privileges of this realm and laws of the same, and in the same manner as has been kept and observed in all Kings' times of Scotland before." At the same time Mary signed this document of Scottish national independence, she signed a different, secret document that stated in the event of her death without an heir, the King of France and his successors would inherit Scotland and her claim to the throne of England. It is probable that Mary did not know at the time that the documents she signed were illegal and could not have foreseen how this document would damage her reputation with her Scottish subjects.

On the 17th November 1558, Mary Tudor, Queen of England, died. Henry VIII's will had already decided the succession of the English throne; should his only son, Edward VI, die without an heir then the throne should descend along the female line of Tudors. The young woman next in line to the English throne after Mary Tudor was Elizabeth Tudor, who had already been declared illegitimate by an Act of Parliament. Elizabeth's illegitimacy was the subject of much debate, as Henry VIII had married Anne Boleyn, Elizabeth's mother, while his first wife, Catherine of Aragon, was still alive. Henry VIII broke from the Catholic Church so that he could "divorce" Catherine and marry Anne, a marriage the Catholic Church never lawfully recognized. Henry himself had repudiated his marriage to Anne when he tired of her and wished to marry again, and had her executed in 1536. For Catholics in England, Scotland, and France, Elizabeth Tudor was not a legitimate heir to the English throne - but Mary Stuart, Queen of Scots, was.

Henry's wishes were made law in the English Parliament approved Act of Succession of 1544, but his preferred line of succession was complicated. If the English throne was to pass down the female line of Tudors then Margaret Tudor, Henry's eldest sister's line, also came into play. Margaret Tudor was, of course, James V's mother and Mary Queen of Scots' grandmother, giving Mary a strong and undeniable claim to the throne. It was only when Queen Mary Tudor died without an heir that it became clear that there was both a Tudor and a Stuart claim to the English throne, and no easy way to decide who the next Queen should be.

Elizabeth was crowned Queen of England on 17 November 1558, but in Paris, this news was met with scorn. Henry II continued with his campaign to have the young King Francis and Queen Mary recognised as the "King and Queen Dauphins of Scotland, England, and Ireland", but the only person who could seriously challenge Elizabeth's claim to the throne was the Pope. King Phillip, freshly widowed from his unhappy marriage to Mary Tudor and desperate to retain his power in England, asked for Elizabeth's hand in marriage, and it was this allegiance that led the Pope to withdraw his public support of Mary. King Philip was too powerful in Italy and the rest of Europe for the Pope to risk offending him.

Mary fell ill in 1559; the exact cause of her illness remains a mystery. There are a number of references to Mary being in poor health throughout her adolescence and later life, but these illnesses were always short-lived. Otherwise in perfect health, it seemed that Mary could be struck down, often at times of great stress, by serious attacks of sickness, breathlessness and, fainting. It is now speculated that Mary was one of a number of royals in her family line to suffer from porphyria, a rare blood disease. Around June 1559, Mary was thought to be so ill she may not live; unbeknownst to all, a different member of the French Royal Family was much closer to death's door.

On the 30th June 1559, King Henry II of France was taking part in a jousting tournament at the Palace of the Tournelles when he was struck in the chest with a lance that slid up his body, under his helmet and into his face. Even the finest surgeons in the land couldn't save Henry, as the lance had struck his brain; he died of a stroke ten days after the tragic accident. Dauphine Francis immediately succeeded his father as King, and Mary, just days from her seventeenth birthday, became the Queen of France.

Meanwhile in Scotland, the Protestant Lords of the Congregation were rising in power. Mary of Guise was still regent but was only able to keep control of her country through the use of French troops. Following the French's capture of Calais, French forces had set about persecuting both English and Scottish Protestants, and Scottish lords were compelled to invite English troops over the border in an attempt to fight back the French. In an attempt to avoid an all-out war, the Guise brothers, acting on behalf of Mary Queen of Scots, who was still in France, negotiated a settlement known as the Treaty of Edinburgh. The treaty forced the English and French troops to retreat from Scotland and recognized Elizabeth as the rightful Queen of England, but Mary refused to sign it - an act of defiance that set the stage for a later stand-off between the warring Queens.

Mary had lost her beloved father-in-law and mother in the space of a year, and now she was set to lose one more important person in her life. In mid-November 1560, King Francis became severely ill with pains in his head. He suffered violent seizures over the next few weeks, and it is speculated that he was suffering from a brain tumour. Francis died on Thursday 5th December 1560 and was succeeded by his brother, Charles IX, who was just ten years old. Where did all this leave Mary?

The relationship between Mary and her mother-in-law, Catherine de' Medici, had grown more and more difficult over the years. Catherine was thought to be jealous of Mary, who was loved by all who met her; following the death of her son, Catherine stood in the way of a union between Mary and her younger son Charles IX, the new King of France. It is thought that Catherine wanted to eradicate the influence of the Guise family in France, and on Mary's first day as a widow, she forced her to hand over every one of her jewels as Queen of France, creating a full inventory that listed every item and its value. Mary then went into a period of solitary mourning that lasted forty days.

Newly widowed, Mary was overwhelmed by offers of marriage from all corners of Europe. The King of Denmark; King of Sweden; the Dukes of Ferrara and Bavaria; Ferdinand I, the Holy Roman Emperor, who was looking for a match for one of his sons; Lord Arran, and Lord Darnley all expressed an interest in Mary, but the main threat came from Spain, where Phillip II was campaigning hard to match Mary with his son, Don Carlos. Mary weighed up her options and decided the best course of action was to return to Scotland.

Chapter Four

Return to Scotland and Marriage to Darnley

"Princes at all times have not their wills, but my heart being my own in immutable."

—Mary Queen of Scots and Queen Consort of France

Mary returned to Scotland and was shocked by the changes that had taken place. A Presbyterian Church government was now in charge. The Protestant Reformation had overthrown the historic Church, seized its properties, ransacked its monasteries, and outlawed its Mass. A Scottish Presbyterian named John Knox was a the heart of the revolution and had published a twenty-five article "Confession of Faith," a document that claimed to outline the correct religious belief and practices of the people of Scotland, and was heavily influenced by the French theologian John Calvin.

John Knox was open in his criticism of the Monarchy and the institutional Catholicism they represented, even publishing a pamphlet entitled "A First Blast of the Trumpet against the Monstrous Regiment of Women" in 1558, a clear attack on Mary Tudor, Queen of England, Catherine de' Medici, Queen Consort of France and Mary de Guise, Queen Regent in Scotland. Knox's opinion on female heads of state was not well-received by the next Queen of England, Elizabeth I, who refused to allow him to return to England, forcing him to settle in Scotland instead.

Mary arrived in Scotland on the 19th August 1561 and is said to have been greeted warmly by most. Although Mary did not seek a counter-revolution to bring Scotland back to Catholicism, she did insist on her own right to worship according to the rites of the Catholic Church. Mary's insistence on taking Mass at the Royal Chapel sparked a riot, and Lord Stewart is said to have stepped in, physically guarding the chapel door against angry rioters who demanded that all "idolatrous priests" be put to death.

Mary began to rely on her half-brother, Lord James Stewart, for advice and support in this country that she ruled but had not seen since she was five years old. While figures such as the Catholic Earl of Huntly offered to raise great armies to return Scotland to its true Catholic faith, Lord Stewart advised Mary adopt a policy of discretion and to take a gentle hand in religious matters. Lord Stewart was a popular and respected politician in Scotland and a sincere convert to the new Presbyterian religion. Mary created him the Earl of Moray in a gesture of thanks, but the relationship between Mary and Moray was complex. Moray was James V's eldest son with his mistress Margaret Erskine and may have resented his illegitimacy, fancying himself a far more worthy king than Mary was a queen.

At the advice of Moray and her secretary of state, William Maitland, Mary committed to a middle way in dealing with the religious divide in Scotland. She publicly accepted the Acts of the Reformation Parliament, which had outlawed Mass, and rode with her army to quash the Catholic rebellion that ensued. Mary's approach, although doubtlessly welcomed by most ordinary people who wished only to worship in their own way without persecution, was not welcomed by staunch Presbyterians like Knox, who saw her tolerance as a weakness.

By December 1561, religious tensions had diminished somewhat, and Mary transformed the Scottish palace into a place of joy, splendor, and magnificence. Transport ships arrived from France packed with Mary's finest treasures. No less than one hundred tapestries were unpacked and used to decorate the walls of the royal apartments and state rooms. Turkish carpets covered the floors, and almost fifty guest rooms were decorated in a style fit for the Queen herself to rest in. The decadence of Mary's palace, her costume, and the velvet and horse-drawn litter that carried her from place to place, were of a sumptuousness never before seen in Scotland. Mary's taste in entertainment, nurtured in France, was also new to the Scottish people; the regular banquets, masques, and dances staged at her palace were the talk of the town.

Now at home in Scotland, it was time for Mary to carefully consider her choice of future husband. Offers of marriage continued to pour in from all corners of Europe, with hopeful suitors looking to rule Scotland alongside the Queen and bring their own political ends to the fore. Queen Elizabeth of England was also keeping a close eye on her cousin's marriage prospects. Resolutely single and famously married only to her country, Elizabeth would never create an heir, and so it was possible that whoever Mary married might one day become the King of England.

In November 1563, Elizabeth asserted a right of veto over Mary's choice of husband and demanded a trial of Mary's dynastic claim. Before these papers landed on Mary's lap, Elizabeth sent her a diamond ring, a token of her affection for her, and just one of many examples of Elizabeth sending Mary mixed messages about the nature of their relationship. A meeting between the "sister Queens" had been on the cards for years, with subtle political machinations constantly getting in the way. Elizabeth is said to have been obsessed with the notion of succession, even forbidding discussion of the matter in her presence, and Mary's marriage was intricately bound up with her own power as a single sovereign.

One of Mary's suitors, the young Earl of Arran, whose father had been regent of Scotland during Mary's childhood in France, believed that Mary had promised him her hand in marriage when they were children. Impatient for the death of Mary's husband, the King of France, Arran had been paying court to Queen Elizabeth, who was not impressed with his duplicitous approach. The rejection of both Queens is said to have driven Arran completely mad, and he spent the remainder of his life in confinement.

Elizabeth's preferred candidate for Mary's future husband was Robert Dudley, Earl of Leicester. An interesting figure, Leicester was rumoured to be Elizabeth's lover and had previously killed his wife to pave his way into the Queen's bed. Mary saw Elizabeth's suggestion that she marry her former lover as a grave insult and refused to have anything to do with Leicester. And then Mary met Darnley.

Lord Darnley was a cousin of both Mary and Elizabeth. Like Mary, Darnley was a grandchild of Margaret Tudor, the sister of King Henry VIII of England, and a descendant of the Stewards of Scotland. Darnley was a few years younger than Mary and said to be handsome, tall, and accomplished in horse riding, fencing, and dancing. The young Queen was head over heels, but Elizabeth did not approve of the match. Darnley had a hereditary claim to the English throne that was second only to Mary, and a union between them would pose a greater threat to Elizabeth's throne than ever before. What's more, Lord Darnley was a Catholic, something that drove a wedge between Mary and her chief advisor Moray, who feared the Roman Catholic Church might again gain dominance in Scotland.

Mary met Darnley for the first time on Saturday, 17th February 1565, at Wemyss Castle in Scotland. Their courtship was swift and passionate, and on the 29th July 1565, they were married at Holyrood Palace, without the papal dispensation necessary for first cousins to marry. Elizabeth was furious, and Mary's refusal to marry her choice of Dudley added another layer of resentment to the relationship between the two Queens that would only intensify in later years.

Moray expressed his anger at the match by raising his Protestant supporters in rebellion of the Queen. Again Mary rode valiantly with her troops, setting out from Edinburgh on 26th August 1565 to confront Moray and his men, and for the next month or two both Mary and Moray roamed around Scotland with their troops, never actually coming to blows.

The scuffle became known as the Chase-about-Raid, and its only important outcome was that it forced Mary to align herself with James Hepburn, Earl of Bothwell, who she made Warden of the Marches. Bothwell appeared to be loyal to Mary, and she trusted him to control the unruly Scottish borderlands, but his reputation preceded him. Bothwell was known to be a violent, ruthlessly ambitious man with Protestant leanings and a scandalous private life. Although educated and fluent in French and Latin, Bothwell had a reputation as a dangerous man, a thug perhaps, and he had many enemies amongst the Scottish and English nobility.

Mary's marriage was a disappointment from the start. Lord Darnley took a mistress in his first few months of marriage, and Mary was disturbed by his taste for "low company" and his frequenting of brothels, including male brothels in Edinburgh. Contemporary historians have also made a case for suggesting Darley was bisexual, a suggestion that, if true, likely added further distress to his new wife. Darnley demanded that he receive the Crown Matrimonial, a title that would give him co-sovereignty over Scotland, and could lead to him becoming King in his own right if Mary died before him. Mary refused to grant Darnley this power, and their marriage became ever more strained.

Mary turned to her confidante in times of need, an Italian man named David Rizzio. David had made the Queen's acquaintance when he travelled with her to Scotland as part of the ambassador for Savoy's entourage. An accomplished musician, the Italian man gave Mary a taste of the refined and elegant culture she missed from her youth in France. Mary made David her secretary, responsible for her correspondence with France, and spent much of her free time with him. Many of Mary's other advisors disliked David, both for his closeness to the Queen and his relationship with the unpopular Darnley. Rumours were spread that David was a papal agent, that his presence in Scotland was a threat to the one true religion of Scottish Presbyterianism, and that he was both Darnley and Queen Mary's lover. Mary became pregnant in October 1565, and Darnley was enraged by the rumour that the father of the child was not him but David Rizzio.

Rumours were also rife that Lord Darnley was plotting against Mary with his father, Lennox. This rumour reached the ears of Moray, who was in exile in England following his failed rebellion and about to lose his extensive estates, and a hasty conspiracy was hatched. Convinced that his wife had become pregnant by another man and desperate for more power, Darnley was easily dragged into the plot. So it was that on the 9th March 1566 Darnley and Moray, with some supporters, took possession of the Palace of Holyroodhouse, Mary's home.

Chapter Five

The Murders of Rizzio and Darnley

"All that is done is the King's own deed and action."

—Lord Ruthven

Darnley led the rebel lords, including Lord Ruthven, who was rumoured to be a warlock, through his private apartments and into the palace. It was around 8 pm, and Mary was in a chamber adjoining her bedroom, enjoying supper with a group of friends that included David Rizzio. Darnley pleaded ignorance of what was about to occur as Lord Ruthven stumbled into Mary's presence and demanded that David come forth. Mary reacted angrily and demanded all of the uninvited guests leave her presence, but violence was on the men's minds, and violence is what they unleashed. A scuffle broke out in which the dining table was overturned. David tried to hide behind Mary to escape his attackers, but they were determined. The conspirators stabbed David to death even as he stood behind Mary, so close she later said she could "feel the cold of the iron" against her skin.

Mary was more than six months pregnant at the time of the assassination and truly believed that the men had come to kill her, too. The leaders of Mary's forces, Bothwell, Huntly and the Earl of Atholl, were also in the palace, and believed their lives to be in danger, but managed to escape. Mary and Darnley then engaged in a venomous row during which it emerged that the main reason Darnley had been complicit in this plot to assassinate Mary's friend was that he felt Mary wasn't doing enough to entertain him in the bedroom.

Mary was being held prisoner in her own chambers, separated even from her ladies in waiting when she frantically penned a number of letters to her most royal supporters seeking out allies. Then, seeing no other choice, she faked a miscarriage to be allowed contact with her ladies. Despite being disgusted by her husband's behaviour and the risk it had posed to her unborn child's life, Mary knew she had to get Darnley back on her side so she could use him against his former allies, who would view his treachery as reason enough to murder him. Now, four years after her return to Scotland, Mary had learned that the only way to defeat her wayward lords was to divide and conquer.

Darnley was full of confidence that he had pulled off a coup against Mary, promising the murderous lords that they would obtain a full pardon in return for their offer of the crown matrimonial at the next meeting of Parliament. After just a few private words with Mary, Darnley was easily convinced to go back on his promises to the Lords and agreed to escape that night. Before dawn, the next morning Mary, Darnley, and a few servants escaped from Holyroodhouse by way of a secret staircase, and then rode for Dunbar, met on the way by a company of Bothwell's soldiers. The ride was hard on Mary, who was heavily pregnant, and she was forced to dismount a number of times to be sick.

Mary stayed at Dunbar for two or three days, during which time the rebellious Lords' plans and allegiances fell apart. Mary offered pardons to a number of rebels involved in the Chase-About-Raid rebellion, providing they distanced themselves from the conspirators who murdered

David Rizzio. For their part, the conspirators were denounced as rebels, proclaimed outlaws, and all their goods were forfeited to the crown.

Early on Sunday 17th March 1566, Mary returned to Edinburgh with her forces, enough to easily occupy the town, and moved into Edinburgh Castle to see out the remaining weeks of her pregnancy in peace. From this time on, Darnley pleaded ignorance and completely denied having any role in the events at Holyroodhouse; the conspirators responded by sending Mary a bond signed by Darnley committing him to the assassination. Even Lennox, Darnley's father, was furious with him for his cowardly actions, and Darnley's life was very much in danger.

On the 19th June 1566, Mary gave birth to a boy who would go on to unite the crowns of Scotland and England as James VI and I. Despite the happiness of bringing a male heir into the world, the marriage between Mary and Darnley was still an unhappy one, and Mary suffered a long period of illness so bad that she drew up a series of wills, bequeathing many of her possessions to her servants.

James was baptized on the 17th December 1566 at six months old. Mary's illness had forced the baptism back, but she had gained strength and was eager to give Prince James a baptism fit for a French king. The three-day event held such glittering excess that the people of Scotland were staggered. The cost of the celebration far exceeded Mary's private means; to pay for the entertainment, she raised taxes and even borrowed money from the merchants of Edinburgh. The baptism was Catholic, and most Protestant Lords boycotted the service, but Queen Elizabeth I was named the child's godmother; she sent a gift of a 333-ounce slab of gold as a show of her dedication to the role.

Darnley sulked and refused to attend the celebrations, a source of major embarrassment for Mary. The possibility of an annulment in her marriage to Darnley was raised, but as soon as it became clear that such proceedings would render James illegitimate, Mary pulled back. Darnley was as eager as Mary to bring the marriage to an end and made fanciful plans to fight in the Spanish Army in the Netherlands or to commission a ship and head to France.

Darnley was incredibly unpopular, not just with his wife and her court but with most of the powerful men in Scotland. That Darnley was a Catholic had not been forgotten, and rumours emerged that he was in commune with the Pope and was planning to assassinate Mary in order to restore the Roman Catholic Church in Scotland. This may seem extreme, but at the time the Roman Catholic Church was gaining more power in Europe, and a counter-reformation was well on its way. A Protestant revolt in the Netherlands was brutally crushed by Spain, and France was on the brink of a civil war. It was more important than ever for Scottish Protestants to assert themselves.

Darnley felt unsafe in Edinburgh, and following the baptism of his son, he retired to Glasgow to live on his father's estates away from his family. Soon after he arrived there he fell ill; poison was suspected, although it is more likely that he simply caught smallpox. Mary herself had contracted smallpox as a child, and so she was able to nurse him without fear of infection. Mary urged Darnley to relocate to Edinburgh, which he did, and she nursed him back to health in the former abbey of Kirk o' Field, just inside Edinburgh's city walls.

It seemed a reconciliation was in the cards as Mary and Darnley were spending hours at a time alone together each day, but on 10th February 1567, tragedy struck. At around 2 AM, a huge explosion destroyed Kirk o' Field. The explosion did not kill Darnley, who was found dead in the garden, some way from the ruined house. Wearing only a nightshirt, the King's body was discovered lying beside that of his valet, apparently strangled or smothered to death.

Mary knew nothing of the murder and was paralyzed with fear that the intended victim of the explosion had been herself. Mary had been sleeping at Kirk o' Field in the weeks previous to the explosion in order to better nurse Darnley. She would have been there that night had she not left around 10 PM, having remembered a promise to dance at the wedding ceremony of one of her servants the next day. It had been planned that Darnley would return with her to Holyroodhouse the next day, and a genuine reconciliation had seemed possible. The mystery of what happened that night at Kirk o' Field, and who was responsible, has never been adequately resolved; immediately following the murder, the finger was pointed directly at Lord Bothwell, the man who owned the house.

Chapter Six

The Final Rebellion

"As the common people say, only harlots marry in May."

—Scottish rhyme

Lord Bothwell was by this time a prominent figure in Mary's life. When Bothwell married Lady Jean Gorden in February 1566, Mary had attended the wedding. It was also believed that in summer 1566, weeks after giving birth, Mary rode through the Borders to see Bothwell at Hermitage Castle, where he was recovering from serious injuries sustained in battle. Bothwell was a friend of Darnley's, but was also referred to as a "godless man" and a willing sword for hire; Lennox, Darnley's father, called for Bothwell to be tried for murder. Meanwhile, placards were being placed around Edinburgh naming Bothwell as a murderer and implying Mary's involvement.

Mary was in a state of despair. Still only 24 years old, Mary had lost her father-in-law, mother, and husband just a few years before; now, over the course of eleven months, she had witnessed her best friend stabbed to death in front of her and her second husband murdered in cold blood. It was likely that members of her own nobility, the men with whom she was supposed to govern her country, had carried out these last two acts of violence; she didn't know who to trust.

Bothwell was brought to trial, and he arrived, willingly, on the 12th April 1657, at the head of a troop of armed men. Lennox had brought a private petition to Mary to force Bothwell to trial, but whether he was afraid of Bothwell, or he simply had no evidence to prove Bothwell's guilt, he failed to launch a case for prosecution. Bothwell was acquitted, but rumors continued to circulate that he had been the murderer.

Now the way was open for Bothwell to pursue his real objective: to win Mary's hand in marriage. For Bothwell to pull this off, he needed not only Mary's consent but the support of the nobility. In a bold move, Bothwell organised a supper at Ainslie Tavern and, intent on winning their support, invited twenty-eight guests from Scotland's nobility, including bishops, earls, and barons. At the end of the meal, Bothwell produced a document that declared that in the event of his marriage to the Queen, those present would fully support him. Most men signed the document, although they would later deny taking part in any such signing.

Bothwell was one of the only men amongst Mary's noble lords who had yet to betray her, and she felt she could trust him. A strong man and a leader, Bothwell seemed to be someone with whom Mary could share the burden of ruling a fractious and divided Scotland. Still, Mary was not in a fit state of mind, and was unable to make a decision that would affect the rest of her life, so when Bothwell proposed, she refused.

Around the 23rd April 1567, Mary visited her son, who was being cared for at Stirling, surrounded by a heavy guard. On her return to Edinburgh, she was abducted by Lord Bothwell and his man and taken to Dunbar Castle, where it is alleged he raped her. Bothwell was at this time still a married man, and he sought a quick divorce so that he could be free to marry Mary. In response, Bothwell's wife, Lady Jean Huntly, accused Bothwell of adultery and asked the court to annul the marriage that had lasted less than a year. It was revealed that the marriage was "null from the beginning in respect of their contingence in blood, without a dispensation obtained before", and both the Catholic Church and the Presbyterian Kirk were in agreement that Bothwell was free to marry again.

On the 15th May 1567, just four months after Darnley's murder, Mary and Bothwell were married. The ceremony was performed under Protestant rites, something Mary seriously regretted after the fact. Mary found neither happiness nor security in this unhappy match, and in the weeks after her marriage, she was said to be in a state of almost constant distress and possibly even suicidal.

The union was unpopular with the public, who were shocked that the Queen would marry the man publicly accused of her husband's murder just months before. A placard was nailed to the gates of Holyrood on the night of the wedding that read, "As the common people say, only harlots marry in May." Catholics were scandalized by the Queen's Protestant service and did not recognise Bothwell's divorce, rendering the union illegal; unsurprisingly, Bothwell's fellow nobles quickly went back on their word to support him.

Bothwell, now the Duke of Orkney and consort of the Queen, could not force his former peers to submit to his authority, and the couple was quickly met with armed rebellion. Twenty-six Scottish peers, known as the confederate lords, rebelled against Mary and Bothwell and raised a formidable army against them. Mary and Bothwell raised an army of their own, riding out to confront the lords at Carberry Hill outside Musselburgh on 15th June, but this army soon dispersed during negotiations, leaving the Queen and her consort completely vulnerable. Mary agreed to submit to the demands of the rebellion if the lords promised safe passage for Bothwell, who quickly left the field.

Mary was now a prisoner of her own people and was taken back to Edinburgh by the Lords who had betrayed her. In Edinburgh, scores of people lined the streets, eager to shout insults at the disgraced Queen. Mary was imprisoned in the Provost's house, forbidden from setting foot inside Holyrood, but the nobles who had staged the uprising and were nervous about what would happen next. Mary still had supporters, among them the powerful Hamiltons, and Bothwell was still at large. It was also understood that the people of Edinburgh were fickle, and Mary's insistence on holding a parliamentary enquiry into Darnley's murder would prove disastrous to the Lords, considering many of them were personally involved.

The Lords decided that Mary should be held somewhere completely secluded, where she would find it impossible to appeal to friends or raise an army of her own. The location chosen was Loch Leven Castle, on an island in the middle of the loch. It is speculated that the only thing that stopped the lords from murdering Mary outright, as they had done David Rizzio and Darnley, was the arrival of Sir Nicholas Throckmorton. Throckmorton had been the English ambassador in Paris when Mary was Queen of France and was sent to Edinburgh by Elizabeth to report on the events. Disgusted by Mary's treatment at the hands of her own lords, Throckmorton reported back to Elizabeth that Mary's life was in danger.

When she entered her isolation in Loch Leven Castle, Mary was already carrying twins. The rebel lords compelled Mary to abandon Bothwell as an outlaw, divorce him and then abdicate in favor of the baby Prince James, who would rule through a regent. Mary refused, hoping that while she was carrying Bothwell's heirs, there was still a chance that all would be well. On the 23rd July, Mary miscarried her twins; the very next day, 24th July 1567, she was forced to sign papers agreeing to her abdication.

Lord Moray, the half-brother she had loved and at one time trusted implicitly, took part in threatening her into signing abdication papers. He forcibly became James' regent, a betrayal that Mary never recovered from. Over time, though she was still incarcerated in Loch Leven, Mary's health began to improve. Unbeknownst to Mary at the time, Bothwell had been driven into exile in Denmark where he was taken prisoner and later died a terrible death, chained to a post in a prison cell. Regardless of the details of his fate, Bothwell was very much out of the picture, unable to return to Scotland and in all likelihood already dead; with this in mind, Mary's resolution returned, and she began to make plans for her future.

The young Queen turned her attention to the chivalrous young men around her. Mary's captor had at least two younger brothers living in the castle; two of them, George and William, fell madly in love with her and plotted her escape. It was boldly done. First, George made up an excuse to leave the island and readied a horse on the mainland. Will then prepared a boat, sabotaged the other boats on the island to hinder any pursuit, and stole the keys to the castle gate. Everything was ready, and all it would take was courage, and a bit of luck, to set the Queen free.

Once darkness fell, Mary slipped out of her room and into the courtyard, where Will was waiting for her. Will rowed Mary to the mainland, where George was waiting on horseback to whisk her away to the home of the Hamiltons, who were awaiting her arrival. The Hamiltons were probably Mary's greatest supporters, not surprising given that the head of the house, the Duke of Chatelherault, was Mary's presumptive heir after Prince James.

With the Hamiltons' help, Mary was able to raise a formidable army that outnumbered that raised by the rebel lords. On the 13th May 1568, the two armies met at Langside, south of Glasgow, in an area now known as Queen's Park. It seemed that Mary had the numbers needed to claim victory, but her army was mismanaged, possibly disloyal, and easily beaten. Again Mary had to flee.

Dumbarton Castle was still being held by her supporters, but to get there, she would be forced to pass through dangerous Lennox-held territory. Instead, Mary headed south-west to Solway Firth.

Chapter Seven

Elizabeth and the Casket Letters

"Burn this letter for it is too dangerous, neither is there anything well said in it, for I think upon nothing but upon grief if you be at Edinburgh."

—Mary Queen of Scots (allegedly) in the Casket Letters.

All of Mary's advisors tried to persuade her to head back to France, her cultural homeland, where she would be safe and might appeal to the French for armed assistance in reclaiming her throne. Mary's mind was made up. She would not travel to France but to England, where she would appeal to her "sister Queen" for help. Mary was confident that, despite their differences, Elizabeth could be trusted to defend her rights as Queen of Scotland and would take her in as a political refugee.

Mary could not have known at this time, as she rode hard through the black Scottish night disguised as an ordinary countrywoman, that a vicious campaign was already underway in England with the aim of ruining her reputation. In England, Mary was now seen as an adulteress and a murderer, intent on forcing Scotland to return to the Roman Catholic Church. From the perspective of Elizabeth's advisors, the tragedy that had befallen Mary ever since she married Darnley was good news. The Catholic Queen had now been replaced by a Protestant coup, and the power France held over Scotland's policies had disintegrated. Elizabeth's advisors saw an opportunity to exploit the new powers in Scotland, who would be relying on England's goodwill for their survival.

Instead of being welcomed warmly in a manner befitting a Queen, Mary was shown to guest rooms and refused an audience with Queen Elizabeth. Elizabeth was playing for time, a characteristic of hers marked upon time and time again by historians, in an attempt to use the situation to her advantage. Moray, Mary's half-brother and chief betrayer, was given the opportunity to explain his actions to Elizabeth before Mary herself was. Moray was well-known and well-regarded by Queen Elizabeth, and the evidence he put before her in defense of his actions became legendary.

Mary was still being treated as a guest in Elizabeth's court when Moray produced what later became known as the "casket letters." The veracity of these letters is incredibly dubious. The original letters disappeared way back in the late sixteenth century and today only clumsy copies remain in English, Scottish and French translations, poorly written and certainly not in the hand of the Queen.

The source of the letters is also problematic. While Mary was enduring her incarceration on Loch Leven, two of the conspiratorial Lords who rebelled and imprisoned her were dining in Edinburgh. They received news that a number of Bothwell's former servants had returned to town and that one of them, a tailor named George Galgleish, was in possession of a silver casket containing letters written by Mary.

The casket letters were incredibly damning for Mary, and Morton sent them to Queen Elizabeth, who appointed commissioners to examine their contents and report back on their findings. According to the commissioners, the letters clearly state that Mary had been committing adultery with Bothwell while her husband Darnley was still alive.

Not content with admitting to adultery, Mary's letters also allegedly reveal that she had foreknowledge of the plot to kill Darnley and was, therefore, complicit in his murder.

Whether or not the casket letters were genuine is a matter still debated by historians today. Was Mary a murderous adulterer or a victim of the designs of powerful men? Most believe the letters to be clumsy forgeries, a suggestion put forward by Moray's secretary John Wood, who asked Elizabeth's council, "If the French originals are found to tally with the Scots translations, will that be reckoned good evidence?" The suggestion is that the Scots versions had already been supplied, and the original French versions could be altered to fit.

Those who would find fortune in Mary's guilt were happy to believe that the casket letters cleared everything up, but Elizabeth was not convinced. If Elizabeth allowed Mary to appear before a tribunal, Mary would undoubtedly deny having written the letters. There was no way to prove that she did, in which case she would be found innocent and would have to be released (even though she was still Elizabeth's "guest"). The only way to manage the situation, as far as Elizabeth's advisors were concerned, was to keep Mary hidden away, deny her a tribunal, and keep the whole thing under wraps.

A second document came to light shortly after the casket letters that was even more disastrous for Mary's reputation, but this took the form of a story written by none other than George Buchanan. At the time of Mary's imprisonment, George Buchanan was the most famous Scotsman in all the land. Buchanan was a scholar, poet, and playwright; and like most at this time, he wrote in Latin. Buchanan was no ordinary poet - his work was said to be second only to Virgil - and worked for a time as the tutor of the Scottish king's illegitimate son Moray, Mary's half-brother.

Mary brought Buchanan back to Scotland with her in 1561. He was the chief intellectual of her court and appointed principal of St. Andrew's University. Importantly, Buchanan had always been Catholic. He was raised Catholic, and had been employed for many years by the extreme-Catholic Royal House of Guise, but in his middle age he switched over to Protestantism, the "one true religion". Buchanan's loyalties were split between Moray and Mary, and he was extremely upset by Darnley's murder, being a fellow Lennox. All of these things combined and led Buchanan to compose Detectio, a beautifully-crafted work of propaganda that confirms the Queen's role in the bloodshed.

The Detectio achieved exactly what its author intended, and convinced many of Mary's guilt; still, Elizabeth would not have her tried for her alleged part in Darnley's murder. Elizabeth detested rebellion, and could hardly endorse the deposition of a fellow monarch but equally had no intention of restoring Mary to her throne. With Moray in charge of Scotland, Elizabeth had a Protestant ally; she put her own interests before that of her poorly-treated cousin.

Chapter Eight

An Incarcerated Queen

"I would never make a shipwreck of my soul by conspiring the destruction of my dear sister."

—Mary Queen of Scots

Elizabeth held Mary prisoner throughout the 1570s and into the 1580s, always denying her the face to face meeting she desperately wanted. Elizabeth treated Mary as a queen, even allowing her to be served by her own household, but her confinement was long and dreary, and Mary spent much time in needlework and fussing over her many pets. Over the years Mary's health worsened, and as she approached her forties, she is said to have looked like a much older woman. Clinging to the hope that her son would gain power and force her release, but ever more secluded from the outside world, Mary turned to her religion for solace.

Beyond the walls of Mary's prison, religious wars raged across Europe. The St. Bartholomew's Night Massacre of 1572, in which French Huguenots were massacred on the streets of Paris, had sent shockwaves around Protestant communities everywhere. Elizabeth had been excommunicated in 1570 and had retorted by making the very existence of Catholic priests illegal. England and Catholic Spain were embroiled in a cold war standoff, and in the Netherlands, a Protestant rebellion against Philip of Spain was turning into a war.

The exact nature of the relationship between Elizabeth and Mary is difficult to define, and further complicated by the fact the two queens never met and only ever communicated through letters or third parties. What is clear is what Elizabeth's advisors, the powerful Lords Cecil and Walsingham, thought about the incarcerated Queen; she was a serious threat and an enemy of England. Elizabeth was nine years older than Mary, and as the years ticked by the men feared Elizabeth may die before Mary. The memory of Mary Tudor's reign and attempt to bring England back to Catholicism was still fresh in the minds of these men; if a Catholic rebellion was to put Mary on the throne of England and Scotland, they knew they would be the first to the gallows.

It took until 1586 for Elizabeth's advisors to finally gather the evidence they needed against Mary to send her to her death. Elizabeth would not agree to Mary's execution unless it were proven absolutely that Mary had plotted to take her life. At the centre of the plot was a young Catholic gentleman named Anthony Babington. Babington, along with a number of other fervent Catholics, had elevated Mary to the status of religious savior and were desperate to free her from her incarceration. The delusional men hatched a fanciful plot to assassinate Elizabeth and restore Mary to the throne, foolishly implicating Mary in the process.

Again, it was letters that served as evidence of Mary's wrongdoing. The veracity of the plot letters, like the casket letters, came under scrutiny in the years following Mary's execution. By 1586, Mary was almost completely cut off from the outside world, and yet somehow Babington's letters made it to her chamber. The letters offered Mary her freedom and, like having a glass of water placed in front of a person dying of thirst, Mary snatched at her opportunity. In one letter to Babington, Mary vaguely assents to his plans, making it clear that he must act quickly and with enough strength to assure her release. It was one statement that may or may not have been written by Mary herself, but it was enough to send Mary to the gallows.

Babington's plot had absolutely no chance of success, and Elizabeth was never in any real danger. Regardless, Babington and his men were rounded up, tortured for their confessions, and executed. Although Mary was given a trial, it was clear that the verdict had already been decided. She stated her case plainly and with spirit, insisting that no English court had any jurisdiction over the Queen of Scotland and the Queen Consort of France.

Mary denied having written anything that proved she was involved in a plot against Elizabeth. In an emotional outburst, she cried, "I would never make a shipwreck of my soul by conspiring the destruction of my dear sister." That said, Mary was an independent Queen, wrongfully held in captivity and from her point of view, even an act of war or treason was legitimate if it granted her freedom. Elizabeth's court did not agree. Mary was that very day sentenced to death.

Chapter Nine

The Execution

"In my end is my beginning."

—Mary Queen of Scots

The final betrayal in a long list of betrayals in Mary's lifetime came from the hand of Elizabeth, her cousin and "sister Queen." For weeks, it was unclear whether Elizabeth would be able to bring herself to sign Mary's death warrant, or whether she would simply keep her incarcerated until one of them died. Elizabeth's own mother, Anne Boleyn, had suffered the ultimate indignity of being beheaded in front of a baying crowd at her father's command. Could she inflict the same horror on Mary? After weeks of soul-searching, Elizabeth came to the conclusion that the only way to protect herself from making the wrong decision was to have Mary quietly murdered before she could be executed.

This was a new low for Elizabeth; this attempt, recorded by the scribes of history, has always left a stain on her character. The man Elizabeth had in mind for the job, Mary's jailer, declined to carry out the gruesome task, saying, "I am so unhappy to have lived to see this unhappy day, in which I am required by direction from my most gracious sovereign to do an act which God and the law forbid... God forbid that I should make so foul a shipwreck of my conscience, or leave so great a blot on my poor posterity, to shed blood without law or warrant."

Shamed by her jailer's refusal to carry out Mary's murder Elizabeth signed the death warrant. Her advisors moved quickly to give her no time to change her mind. In the weeks leading to her execution, Mary is said to have been in good spirits, perhaps disbelieving that her ordeal would end in actual execution. Then, on the 4th February 1587, three of Elizabeth's earls arrived at Mary's apartments at Fotheringhay Castle and informed her that she would be executed shortly after eight o'clock the following morning.

In response, Mary thanked the earls for the "good news." Tired of incarceration, and convinced that no more could be done to assist her in her cause, Mary adopted the position of martyr and assured that she would never be forgotten by followers of the Catholic faith. "I am quite ready and happy to die," she said, and to shed my blood for Almighty God, my Saviour and my Creator, and for the Catholic Church, and to maintain its right in this country."

That night Mary wrote her will, set about distributing her possessions amongst her loyal staff, and penned a number of letters, the last of which she sent to King Henry III of France, whom she had known since he was born. The next morning she readied herself for execution with the help of her servants, donning the auburn wig that nobody knew hid her thin, grey hair underneath, and a lavish black silk gown. Summoned by the local sheriff of Nottinghamshire close to eight AM, Mary walked, an ivory crucifix in one hand and her prayer book in the other, towards her death.

The events of Mary's execution have become legend. In a bizarre standoff, Mary and her servants recited Catholic prayers in Latin while the Protestant executioners countered with Christian prayers in English. When Mary was finally undressed for execution, she stood before a shocked crowd in underclothes in the colour of dried blood, the liturgical colour of martyrdom in the Roman Catholic Church. The executioner, no doubt in a state of extreme stress, botched his first attempt at removing Mary's head with an axe and had to strike her three times to complete the deed. On lifting Mary's decapitated head to the crowd, the Executioner dislodged her wig, revealing her grey hair and true appearance to the spectators. In a final, gruesome twist, Mary's favorite dog, who had been hiding in the folds of her dress throughout, emerged and lay in a thick pool of blood at her severed neck and refused to move. The execution was never forgotten by any soul who witnessed it and has gone down in history as one of the most shocking and macabre displays in the history of the British monarchy.

Conclusion

To the very end, Mary had stood by her hereditary right to the English throne, wishing only to be recognised as Elizabeth's successor, and in a way she succeeded. Queen Elizabeth died on the 24th March 1603 and famously refused to the very end to name her successor. Elizabeth's wishes unknown or disregarded, James I was proclaimed King of England and Ireland on the back of a proclamation that declared his right to the crown by "lineal succession and undoubted right." Mary is not mentioned, but the meaning of the proclamation is clear: Mary was always the rightful successor to Queen Elizabeth's throne in the eyes of the law. Every subsequent ruler of Great Britain to this day is descended from Mary Queen of Scots and not Elizabeth, who died the "Virgin Queen."

James I had rejected his mother during her incarceration and did little to free her. Once he became King, James set about atoning for his behavior and commissioned the building of two magnificent monumental tombs at Henry VII's chapel at Westminster Abbey, one for Elizabeth and one for Mary. James also encouraged a well-respected historian, William Camden, to write the Annals of Elizabeth's reign, a document that served to repair much of the damage that had been done to Mary's reputation during her lifetime.

Mary was an enigmatic queen. Beautiful, vivacious and courageous, she was loved by all who knew her but was a victim of circumstance time and time again, betrayed by almost every influential person in her life. Mary's fairy-tale upbringing and early adulthood in France came to a tragic end when her father-in-law, husband, and mother all died within a few years of each other; from then on Mary swapped the sunny, carefree days of life in France with the grey skies and murderous politics of Scotland. A number of poor choices, particularly when it came to husbands, forced Mary down the wrong path and embroiled her in a series of unfortunate events that ultimately led her straight into Elizabeth's jealous hands.

A queen in every fiber of her body and soul, Mary may have ended her life as a victim, but in death she rose magnificently from the flames, writing her own epitaph, "In my end is my beginning."

Made in the USA
Monee, IL
15 December 2022

21931814R00026